Old Bear Tales

Old Bear Tales

This edition published by Blitz Editions 1992
an imprint of Bookmart Limited
Registered Number 2372865
Trading as Bookmart Limited
Desford Road, Enderby, Leicester LE9 5AD

Originally published in 1988 by
Hutchinson Children's Books
an imprint of Random House UK Ltd
20 Vauxhall Bridge Road, London SW1V 2SA

Printed in Hong Kong

ISBN 1 8560 5124 2

Old Bear Tales

JANE HISSEY

For Molly and Betty
and with many thanks to everyone
who lent me their bears

CONTENTS

THE DOLLS'-HOUSE CHRISTMAS

Christmas had nearly arrived. The toys all knew this because the children were very busy decorating the house. They were too busy to play and they wouldn't let the toys help with the decorations. 'How can you decorate the Christmas tree?' they said to Little Bear. 'You'd get prickles in your fur. And how could you hang paper chains,' they said to Rabbit. 'You couldn't reach.'

They wouldn't let Old Bear help with the holly or Duck put up the fairy lights. It really wasn't much fun at all for the toys. 'We haven't been able to do anything,' grumbled Little Bear. 'I would have loved to help make the house look Christmasy.'

'They could have saved the low-down jobs for us,' said Rabbit.

'What low-down jobs?' said Old Bear. 'There aren't any really, are there?'

'There's the pot the Christmas tree stands in,' said Little Bear, 'that's low down and it's always decorated.'

They all rushed to the Christmas-tree pot only to find that it had just been wrapped in red crêpe paper and tied with a big green bow. 'Oh well, that's that, then,' said Little Bear. 'Now there's nothing left for us to do.'

It was then that he noticed the dolls' house. Standing in the corner of the playroom, it had been completely forgotten. There were no paper chains in the rooms, no Christmas tree with presents underneath, and no holly over the pictures. It looked just as it did all the rest of the year.

'Why haven't you decorated the house?' Little Bear asked the dolls'-house dolls. 'It doesn't look very festive.'

'We haven't any decorations,' said one of the dolls. 'Nobody really bothers with the dolls' house at Christmas time. They're too busy doing other things.'

'Oh, that's wonderful,' said Little Bear. 'We'll decorate it for you. It's just what we wanted. We can reach into every corner of the dolls' house and we'll make the decorations ourselves.'

The other toys were very excited at Little Bear's

idea and, very soon, they were off in search of suitable decorations.

Old Bear was the first to find something. He arrived at the dolls' house carrying a tiny but perfect Christmas tree. 'I found it in the dustbin – it's a little branch that had broken off the big tree,' he explained, 'but it's just the right size for the dolls' house.'

They planted the tiny tree in a little egg cup with soil packed tightly round its stem to stop it wobbling.

'It needs fairy lights,' said the biggest doll. 'What can we use?'

Rabbit rummaged through the button and beads box until he found what he was looking for: some tiny, coloured, glass beads. He threaded them on a piece of green cotton and wound them in and out of the branches of the tree. When the light caught them, they did look just like fairy lights and the dolls'-house dolls were delighted. They found other beads to hang on the tree as decorations and Little Bear stuck a tiny, gold, sticky-paper star on top.

‘Well that’s the tree done,’ said Old Bear. ‘Now for the rest of the house.’

Little Bear couldn’t find any holly small enough for the dolls’ house so he cut holly-leaf shapes out of green paper and they used these to decorate the mirrors and to make a Christmas holly wreath for the front door.

Rabbit sat and cut up very thin strips of wrapping paper and all the toys used these to make dolls’ house-sized paper chains. Then, Old Bear, who could comfortably reach into every corner of the house, hung the paper chains up so they criss-crossed all the tiny rooms. The dolls’ house was really looking ready for Christmas now and the toys all began to feel excited.

‘We’ll put our presents under the tree now, shall we?’ suggested Rabbit. They had all wrapped presents up to give each other – little things they’d made or found. They piled these up in a heap under the tree.

And, as the finishing touch, one of the dolls rushed off and returned with all the doll-sized socks

she could find. 'We'll all have to have bare feet until Christmas,' she laughed, 'but we don't mind. There are enough socks here for everyone.' And she hung the socks in a row along the dolls'-house mantelpiece.

'Now the house looks like a real house,' said Little Bear, as he stood back to admire all their work. 'And it has been fun decorating it.'

And do you know, on Christmas morning, when the dolls'-house dolls walked into their sitting room they could hardly believe their eyes, for every tiny sock was full of tiny presents. So they hadn't been forgotten after all, had they?

SUNSHINE SAM AND THE SPECIAL PRESENT

It was Christmas Eve and Sunshine Sam, the yellow bear, sat with the other toys. They were watching the children wrapping each others' presents in bright paper.

'We were all presents once,' said Tom Ted. 'It was lovely, wasn't it? First we were wrapped up in pretty paper and tied round with bright ribbons, then, on Christmas morning, we would feel the ribbon being untied and we would hear excited voices . . . .'

'And then we would jump out and meet all the other toys,' said Sunshine Sam.

'And play with all the games and be hugged and taken out for walks,' said Tom Ted.

'I'd like to be a present again,' said Sunshine Sam. 'It would be lovely to be a surprise for someone.'

'But nobody would be surprised by you now!' said Tom. 'The children would just be disappointed because you aren't new.'

'I'd still like to try,' said Sam.

'Well you can't do it on your own,' said Tom. 'I suppose I'd better help.'

When the children went to bed, Sam and Tom hid behind the curtains. Everyone looked everywhere for them and they nearly came out when they saw how worried the children were at bedtime. 'We wanted them in our beds,' said the little girl, Amy. 'Christmas won't be the same if we can't find Sam and Tom.'

'They'll turn up,' said Mummy and Daddy. 'Don't worry; they can't be far away.'

With their paws tucked up in the curtains, Sam and Tom waited and waited for Mummy and Daddy to go to bed too. Mummy was busy hanging up Christmas cards and Daddy was making paper chains. By the time they'd gone to bed, the two bears had given up waiting and had fallen asleep. It was still dark when they woke up because it was very, very early in the morning.

Tom peeped out from behind the curtain. 'Oh Sam, Father

Christmas has been already,' he said. 'The stockings are all lumpy with presents.'

'Will there still be room for me?' asked Sam.

'Of course there will,' said Tom. 'Come on, it's time to wrap you up.'

The two bears crept over to where the wrapping paper was kept and chose the brightest, prettiest paper they could find.

'Will it fit?' asked Sam. 'I don't want my paws to stick out.'

'It looks fine,' said Tom. 'Come on, we must hurry, it's getting lighter every minute.'

Sam chose the ribbon next – a bright, shiny red one. 'Look, Tom, isn't this lovely,' he said, stroking it with his paw.

'Yes,' said Tom, 'and it is time I was tying you up with it. Hurry now if you want to be a present, the children will soon be down to see what's in their stockings.'

Sam and Tom carefully climbed up to the top of one of the stockings, carrying with them the paper and the lovely red ribbon. Soon they found a little space between a long, thin parcel and a flat, square one.

'Right Sam,' said Tom, 'lie down on the paper and roll yourself up in it.'

Sam stretched out on the wrapping paper and

Tom helped to roll him over and over. It was difficult because they kept bumping into the long thin parcel. Soon, however, Sam began to look more like a present and less like a bear. Now it was time for the ribbon.

'Are you ready?' called Tom.

Sam's muffled voice came through the layers of paper, 'Tie me up, I'll really be a present then.'

Tom folded over the ends of the paper and wrapped the red ribbon around Sam's tummy. Then he tied a lovely bow.

'Have you finished?' called a muffled Sam.

'Yes, you're all ready,' said Tom, tucking the bear-shaped parcel into the top of the stocking. 'See you later, Sam.' He climbed carefully down and settled himself on the sofa to wait for the children. He didn't have long to wait; in less than an hour the children rushed into the room.

'He's been, he's been,' they cried when they saw the bulging stockings. Just look at all the presents.'

They lifted the stockings down and laid them on the sofa. It was then that they saw Tom. 'Tom Ted,' they cried, 'you're here after all. We did so want you to share the fun, but we still haven't found Sunshine Sam – Christmas just won't be the same without him.'

The first parcel to be opened was the long thin one, which had been tucked in next to Sam. 'It's a little umbrella,' cried Amy. 'Oh Sam would have loved this umbrella, he could have gone for walks with me in the rain and kept his fur dry.'

The next present was the flat one on the other side of Sam. 'Oh look,' cried Amy, 'it's a lovely book. I could have snuggled down in bed with Sam to read this but now I can't because he's lost.'

She wiped a tear away and then reached into the stocking for the third parcel. This time it was Sam's parcel. She took hold of it and carefully lifted it out. 'What pretty ribbon,' she said, smiling. 'I wonder what's inside.'

She undid the ribbon and pulled back the wrapping paper. 'Sunshine Sam!' she cried. 'It's you! You aren't lost. But how did you get in there? Perhaps Father Christmas found you and brought you home. Oh I'm so happy! You're the best present I've ever had!'

And she tied the lovely red ribbon round Sam's neck in a big, bright bow, and she showed him her umbrella and her book. 'Come on, Sam,' she said, 'let's open the rest of the presents together.'

'You see, Tom,' said Sam later on, when they were sitting quietly amidst the sea of wrapping paper, 'the children really did like me being a present again. Amy said I was the best one that she has ever had.'

'Yes,' said Tom Ted, 'that's true, but I don't think you'd better try it again. I think being a surprise twice is quite enough.'

The Winter Picnic

Spring had not quite arrived; there were no leaves on the trees or eggs in the nests and all the toys were well wrapped up and sitting around in the playroom.

'Let's go for a picnic,' said Old Bear, suddenly.

'A picnic?' chorused the others. 'But it's cold.'

'Then we'll take warm food and coats,' said Old Bear. 'It's a perfect day for a picnic.'

'Why is it perfect?' asked Bramwell Brown, looking at the trees blowing in the wind outside.

'Because nobody else will be having a picnic,' said Old Bear, 'so we'll be able to choose the best picnic place and have it all to ourselves.'

'And nobody else will be using the picnic basket,' said Little Bear.

'Or the blanket,' added Bramwell Brown.

'That's right,' said Old Bear, getting to his feet.

'Come on, everyone, let's get ready.'

Old Bear filled a hot-water bottle and put it in the bottom of the picnic basket. Then he put everything else in on top. He made the sandwiches with hot toast, and wrapped them up and put them right on top of the hot-water bottle to keep warm. Then he filled a flask with hot soup and wrapped up hot buns, sausage rolls, baked potatoes in their jackets and a jar of honey. He packed a few other bits and pieces while the others fetched blankets, coats and jumpers. Soon they were all ready.

There was just a hint of frost on the path as they marched out of the house, dragging the picnic basket along on a little four-wheeled cart.

'We must be mad!' said Bramwell Brown. 'But it's rather fun to be having the first picnic of the year. Where are we going to have it?'

'I suggest over there,' said Old Bear, pointing to the top of a little hill. 'It will be a nice view up there.'

'It'll be a bit windy,' said Harry Bear, rather doubtfully. 'And we'll have to walk all the way back, don't forget.'

But nobody was really listening; they were pulling and puffing their way up the hill. By the time they were halfway up, most of them had taken off their coats and some had even removed their jumpers. Harry Bear took off his scarf.

'I feel quite warm again now,' said Bramwell, 'and I'm very hungry.'

At last, they reached the highest point. 'This will do,' said Old Bear, spreading out one of the blankets and sitting down in the middle of it. The others joined him. They left the basket on the little path and unloaded the food. The soup in the flask was lovely and warm and they all wrapped their paws around a steaming mug of it. The honey had gone a bit runny and the butter had melted out of the sandwiches, but it all tasted good; in fact, everything tasted especially good and, in no time at all, the food had all gone.

But when they'd finished, the toys began to shiver again. 'Come on,' said Old Bear, 'it's too cold to sit still – let's play some games.'

They played a very quick game of 'hide and seek' and an even quicker game of 'hunt the acorn' and then they rolled pebbles down the hill. Rolling pebbles down the hill wasn't really active enough and, soon, they began to feel chilly again.

'The hot-water bottle is still warm in the picnic basket,' said Bramwell Brown. 'Why don't we all get in with it for a little while, just for a warm up!'

Rubbing their paws together they all climbed into the nearly-empty basket.

'Oh . . lovely,' said Harry Bear, as his paws touched the warm hot-water bottle. 'I'm as warm as summer time, now.'

They all snuggled down while Old Bear told them stories of picnics he used to go on when he was a new bear many years ago. They didn't mind that the basket was a bit sticky with spilt honey, or that there were crumbs all over their fur. 'It's warm in here, isn't it,' said Little Bear. 'I won't want to get out to go home.'

None of them wanted to get out but, as it turned out, they didn't actually have to. They had forgotten that the picnic basket was still on the little four-wheeled cart. Suddenly a big gust of wind caught the open lid and began to blow the basket down the hill. 'Oh no!' cried Old Bear. 'Help!'

But of course there was nobody to help. Nobody else was out having picnics in weather like that. They were the only ones. All they could do was hold on to each other as tightly as they could and hope that the basket wouldn't stop too suddenly.

'It's when things like this happen,' said Bramwell Brown, shakily, 'that you wish you were having a picnic on a normal sort of day when there were lots of people around to rescue you.'

The basket bumped its way on down the little

hill. It jumped a very small stream and headed towards the gate. 'Duck!' shouted Old Bear.

And they all ducked, except Little Bear who was busy *looking* for a duck as they whizzed under the bottom rung of the gate. If anyone had seen the picnic basket now, they would have thought it was just a picnic basket on wheels rolling down the hill. They would never have guessed that there were five brave picnickers inside.

'Oh, when is it going to stop?' asked Little Bear.

'When it gets to the bottom, I should think,' said Bramwell Brown. And he was more or less right. The little cart suddenly hit a log; the basket fell off the cart and the five friends fell out of the basket. When they realized that they weren't moving any more, and dared to look, they found that they were right outside their own front door.

'Well, isn't that wonderful,' said Little Bear, 'a picnic on top of a hill and we didn't even have to walk back.'

'I think perhaps I would rather have walked back,' said Old Bear, standing up rather shakily, 'but for the first picnic of the year, that's going to be hard to beat.'

'Yes,' said Bramwell Brown, 'travelling home from the picnic isn't usually the most exciting bit, is it?'

And gathering up the basket, its contents, and the little cart, they all trooped indoors for tea!

WET BEAR

Barnaby Bear stood on the doorstep feeling cold and damp. What a day to be left out in the rain. How could they have forgotten that he'd been in the garden. It just wasn't fair. He was still standing there gazing out at the rain when Teddy George came into the kitchen. 'Oh dear,' he said. 'What happened to you?'

'I was out in the garden and I fell asleep,' said Barnaby. 'Nobody took me in when it started raining and I'm so wet and cold. How can I get warm and dry?'

'The best thing to do is run around,' said George. 'That always warms you up.'

Barnaby Bear began to run up and down the kitchen. 'Like this?' he puffed, as he passed George for the fifth time.

'Yes, that's the way,' said George. But just as he said it, Dog came through a door and collided with Barnaby. They both landed in a heap.

'Why were you running?' asked Dog.

'To keep warm,' said Barnaby.

'Oh, you'd do better to wrap up in something,' said Dog. Dog and

Teddy George fetched a sheet and wrapped Barnaby up in it. 'Do you feel warmer now?' they called.

The sheet had been a rather large one and they couldn't actually see Barnaby any more. 'I feel warmer,' came the muffled reply, 'but I can't see where I'm going.' And he staggered across the room, trying not to trip over his feet.

Hearing all the muffled voices, Little Bear came trotting in through the door. He shrieked when he saw a lumpy, flapping sheet staggering across the room towards him. 'A ghost, a ghost!' he cried, and rushed to hide behind Teddy George.

'No, it's all right,' called the ghost. 'It's only me, Barnaby. I'm trying to wrap up to keep warm. I got wet in the garden.'

'Why don't you just jump up and down,' said Little Bear. 'But not dressed up as a ghost,' he added.

'All right,' said Barnaby, throwing off the sheet and jumping up and down. 'You're right. I am getting warmer, but I can't keep doing this 'til my fur's dry.'

'No,' said Teddy George, 'you can't. You're

making the plates rattle. I tell you what, I saw a hot-water bottle at the back of this cupboard one day; I could fill it with warm water from the tap. That will warm you up.' Teddy George rummaged about and found the old hot-water bottle. He took it to the tap and filled it with warm water. 'There,' he said to Barnaby, 'feel that.'

A happy smile spread across Barnaby's face as he hugged the warm hot-water bottle close to his fur. 'Oh, it's lovely,' he said. 'Thank you, Teddy George.'

Then the smile slowly left his face. 'George,' he said, slowly and thoughtfully, 'I think I know why nobody uses this hot-water bottle any more. It leaks.' He carefully laid the hot-water bottle on the ground and looked down at his fur. It was wetter than ever. Warm and wet this time.

'Oh no,' chorused the others.

'Newspaper,' said George, 'that's what we need.'

Dog rushed off and returned with the newspaper.

'Now,' said George, opening up the newspaper, 'you lie on that, Barnaby, and we'll roll you up in it. Newspaper keeps you warm and dry.'

With the help of the others, Teddy George rolled Barnaby up in the newspaper until he looked like a sausage roll.

Jane Hissey

'Now what?' said Barnaby, with only his head sticking out of the newspaper roll.

'Now we wait,' said Teddy George, sitting down.

'You can't leave me like this,' wailed Barnaby.

'We'll let you out when you're dry,' said Dog.

'But I want to get out now,' said Barnaby, rolling around the floor like a cross rolling pin. He tripped Little Bear up and then Dog, and then they all bumped into George. Soon, there was a great heap of toys in the middle of the floor. Barnaby wriggled out of the newspaper and out from under the heap. He looked at Dog with his feet in the air and George with Little Bear sitting on his middle and he began to laugh. He laughed and laughed. 'Do you know,' he said, 'all that rolling around has completely dried my fur and laughing is a wonderful way to warm up. I think I shall know what to do now if I ever get left out in the rain again.'

Katie Camel and the Desert Party

Katie Camel was miserable. Everyone had tried to cheer her up but she still seemed miserable. Little Bear had spent nearly a whole morning standing on his head, trying to make her laugh. Bramwell Brown had gone through his entire collection of jokes and Old Bear had made her breakfast in bed.

'Why are you so miserable?' asked Little Bear, at last, when he had stopped standing on his head.

'I feel lonely,' said Katie, as she nibbled sadly at a piece of Old Bear's toast. 'I had a lovely dream last night. I dreamt that I was in the desert all night. The sky was full of stars and I was playing in the sand with lots of other camels. And then I woke up,' she added sadly, 'and I found I wasn't in the desert, I was here, and it's very disappointing when one minute you're in the desert and the next, you're not. And one minute, there are lots of camels and the next, there aren't.'

'Yes,' said Little Bear, 'I expect it is. Never mind, you've got us.'

'Umm,' said Katie, doubtfully, 'but you're not much like camels, are you?'

'Er, I suppose not,' said Little Bear.

Little Bear left Katie staring sadly at a picture of a palm tree she had found in a book, and went to tell the others why she was so miserable.

'Oh dear,' said Old Bear. 'But don't worry, Little Bear, I think I have an idea.' He gathered all the toys together and whispered his plan. Soon, the whole playroom was a hive of activity. One group of toys seemed to be painting something big, and another group had needles and thread and were sewing pieces of material.

Bramwell Brown had gone out to the garden on some secret errand. Later on, when Old Bear said everything was ready, they all went to collect Katie. Katie had been so busy being miserable, that she hadn't noticed anything going on at all.

'Now Katie, we have a surprise for you,' said Old Bear, 'but we don't want you to see it until

we get you there, so I'm going to blindfold you.' Carefully, he pulled a woolly hat down over Katie's eyes so she couldn't see where she was going. Then, he led her down the stairs and out into the garden. Once there, he said, 'All right, you can look now,' and he pulled off the woolly hat.

They were standing on the edge of the sandpit, but oh, how different it looked! All around the edge were cardboard cut-out palm trees that the toys had carefully painted to look like real ones. The sand had been raked smooth to look like the desert and all the toys were dressed up as camels. Some had proper camel suits on that they'd made and others had put on coats and jumpers and had ping-pong balls inside their jumpers to look like humps. Some had one hump, because they were dromedaries, some had two humps, and one rather forgetful little teddy had three humps because he'd lost count.

'It's a desert party,' said Old Bear, 'and you are the very special guest, Katie.'

Katie stared in amazement at the sandpit desert and all the teddy-bear camels and then she began to laugh, and soon she was rolling about in the sand laughing. 'Oh, Old Bear,' she said, when she could find the breath to speak, 'this really has cheered me up. How could I mind about a dream now. All my friends are real and they make wonderful camels.'

And that night, everyone was very late to bed. They were all out in the sandpit dancing and singing by the light of the moon and the stars. Katie Camel still sometimes dreams about playing with the camels in the desert, but now the dream doesn't make her miserable. It reminds her of the surprise desert party and all her very kind friends.

THE BUNNY DANCER

Lizzie Long-ears loves to dance
With music or without it,
And if she ever gets a chance
She'll tell you all about it;
She'll mention that she leaps and lands
On just one toe and stays there
(She balances so perfectly
She might spend several days there!)
She pirouettes and hops and jumps,
And if you've ever seen her
You'll know without a doubt that
She's a bunny ballerina.

There Were Four in the Bed

Old bear woke with a bump when something hit him on the head. 'Don't do that,' he said, crossly, and then opened his eyes and found he was talking to the floor. 'Well, I wonder how I got down here,' he muttered, rubbing his head with his paw.

'You fell out of bed,' said a voice from above him.

Looking up, he saw a row of faces staring down at him:

Bramwell Brown the bear, Lucy the rabbit, and Duck.

'If you ask me,' said Duck, 'there are too many toys in this bed. It's overcrowded.'

'Well, it isn't too bad now,' said Lucy, 'not now that Old Bear has gone.'

'But I haven't gone!' said Old Bear.

'You look as though you have,' said Lucy, hanging dangerously over the side to see how far down Old Bear was.

'Well, I didn't mean to go,' said Old Bear. 'It just happened.'

'If a few more people happen to go,' said Duck, thoughtfully, 'the others would be able to spread out.'

'Are you hurt?' asked Bramwell Brown.

'Well, I did bump my head,' said Old Bear, glad that someone cared.

Bramwell Brown climbed down and bandaged his old friend's head with a handkerchief. 'Is that better?' he asked, kindly.

'Yes, thank you,' said Old Bear. 'You know, perhaps it is true that the bed is too crowded; I think I'll try and find somewhere else to sleep.'

'We could all look for somewhere else,' said Bramwell. 'It would be nice to have a change.'

The others climbed down too, and all four of

them set off to look for a new bed. The first place they found was an open drawer. 'This looks really good,' said Lucy Rabbit, climbing in. 'It's full of socks.'

'They're nice and soft,' said Bramwell Brown. 'I could sleep in here very comfortably.'

'And what would happen if someone shut the drawer?' asked Duck.

'Oh dear, I hadn't thought of that,' said Lucy, wriggling out of the drawer as fast as she could. 'I wouldn't want to be stuck in there forever.'

'No, drawers are not a good idea,' said Old Bear.

Bramwell Brown found a large fruit basket, next. 'I think this would be good,' he said, 'except that it's half full of fruit.'

'Oh, we could easily eat that,' said Lucy, who was always hungry, and she began to munch a large apple. Some hours later, the fruit basket was empty. Well, it was empty of fruit. Instead, four rather full toys sat in it where the fruit had been.

'It's big enough,' said Old Bear.

'But it's not very comfortable,' added Duck.

'We could come and sit in it for a change,' said Bramwell Brown, 'perhaps when we're

hungry. But I don't think we could sleep here.'

'I'm so full, I could sleep anywhere,' said Lucy.

But the others dragged her out of the basket and continued to search. Lucy was soon busy pulling the cushions off all the chairs and piling them in a great heap on the floor. 'Come on, everyone,' she called from the top. 'Try it out.'

The cushions were so bouncy it made them hard to climb up but, eventually, they were all balanced on the top.

But the cushions wouldn't stay still, and soon Old Bear found himself on the floor once more.

'Oh my poor head,' he said, rubbing his bandage. 'I'm sure I keep bumping my head just because it's already been bumped. I'm going to take off my bandage.'

'We could use that handkerchief,' said Lucy, 'it would make a hammock.'

Lucy Rabbit and Bramwell Brown put the hanky hammock up between two chair legs. Old Bear decided he'd never get into a hammock, especially with someone else, and he set off for the kitchen. He'd remembered he'd seen a very comfortable looking basket there which was lined with straw and used to keep eggs in. It could be just the thing. When he arrived in the kitchen, he climbed up and settled himself in the straw like a rather

Jane Hissey

strange chicken. What luxury, he thought. If there hadn't been five eggs in the basket, there might even have been room for him to lie down. But there were five eggs, and he wasn't a chicken, so he couldn't sit on the eggs. His paws seemed to get in the way. And just as he was climbing out of the egg basket, he heard a crash. 'Oh no! What's happened now,' he said, rushing back to the other room. And there he found his friends – under the handkerchief hammock.

'It wasn't strong enough for all of us,' said Lucy. 'We fell out.'

'Do you know, I think our bed was the safest place, after all,' said Old Bear, 'but I've had an idea how we can have more room.'

And that night, if you'd peeped into their room, you would have seen Duck, Lucy Rabbit and Bramwell Brown tucked up in their usual place in bed. But down at the other end of the bed, tucked in the other way round, so his paws met theirs in the middle, was Old Bear. He had the whole end of the bed to himself and he looked very comfortable and very safe.

Flossie and Ginger at the Seaside

It was a hot summer's day and Ginger and Flossie, the two teddy bears, were on holiday at the seaside with the children. They'd all been playing hide and seek in the towels and rolling down sand hills, but now the children were going into the sea for a swim. 'You guard our buckets and spades,' they said to the bears, 'we'll be back later to build sand castles.' And with that, they skipped over the wet sand and into the waves.

'I wish we could swim,' said Ginger. 'I'm so hot under all my fur.'

'Perhaps we could cool down in the sand,' said Flossie. 'Let's build a sand castle big enough to get inside.'

The two bears set to work at once. They dug and dug. They filled the bucket over and over again to build tower upon tower. Then, while Ginger worked at the castle, Flossie dug a deep moat round it and joined it to the sea with a long canal. It filled up with water every time a wave

came in and the whole thing looked just like a real castle. Flossie and Ginger put four towers on the four corners and then made the towers look like four teddy bears with pebbles for eyes and noses and shells for ears.

'We'll call our castle "Teddy Towers",' they said, and wrote it in the sand.

'Phew, I'm really hot now,' said Flossie.

'The castle is nearly big enough to get into,' said Ginger, 'just one more spadeful.' But as Ginger pushed his spade in for the last time, it hit something hard. With his paws, he dug down to see what it was and came up with a ten-pence piece.

'Oh whoopee!' cried Flossie. 'We can go and buy ice creams now – I'm boiling.'

'That's a very good idea,' said Ginger. 'I'll finish this off while you go to the ice-cream man.'

Flossie marched happily up the beach, carrying the ten-pence piece. She found the ice-cream man standing by the heap of deck chairs. She knew it was the ice-cream man because he had a sign saying: NICE COLD ICE CREAMS – 10p each. Flossie looked at the money in her paw – it was ten pence – that meant she could only buy one ice cream with her money. Oh dear! One ice cream would never be enough

to cool down two hot bears. Still, it had to be better than no ice cream. So she marched over and offered her money.

She arrived back at Teddy Towers, carefully carrying the precious ice cream, and explained to Ginger that ice creams were ten pence each. They were just about to decide who would have the first lick when a man and a woman came over to them. 'Excuse me,' they said, 'we have just come to tell you that you have won the "best sand castle on the beach" competition.

Flossie and Ginger stared in amazement. They hadn't even known there was a competition. 'Thank you,' they said, 'how exciting!'

'And your prize', said the woman, 'will be an ice cream each for every day of your holiday. Here is today's prize.' And she handed Flossie two more ice-cream cones.

'Goodness!' laughed the bears when the people had gone. 'A little while ago we had no ice creams, and now we've got three. What shall we do?'

'Well, I know what I'm going to do,' said Flossie, and she sat down in front of Teddy Towers to enjoy her prize.

And I think they were so hot they managed all three ice creams, don't you?

HENRY ISAIAH

Henry Isaiah was a bear. He was called Henry Isaiah because one eye was higher than the other one. He had been called Henry Isaiah for as long as he could remember, and for as long as he could remember he had wished he was called something else.

'Do you think I ever had another name?' he asked his friend Rags one day.

'Well, I suppose if your eyes were straight when you were new, Isaiah would have been a silly name,' said Rags. 'Perhaps you were called something else then.'

'I wish I had a nice short name like yours,' said Henry Isaiah.

'You wouldn't want to be called Rags would you?' said Rags. 'I think it means I look like a rag-bag with bits of material mending my paws. I was a smart new bear once, but I've been hugged until I'm threadbare. I can't always have been called Rags, but nobody remembers the name I had when I was new. If you want to find someone who will remember your old name,

you'd better ask Furless Fred. He's even older than me and he remembers us all when we were new.' Henry Isaiah found Furless Fred sitting in the garden amongst the flowers.

'Furless,' said Henry Isaiah, 'was I always called Henry Isaiah?'

'I think so,' said Furless. 'Your eyes were like that when you were new – one up and one down.'

'But it's such a silly name,' said Henry Isaiah.

'Not as silly as Furless Fred,' said Furless Fred. 'I was just called Fred once, but I've been left in the garden so many times now all my fur is worn off and everyone calls me Furless.'

'Well, if I never had a better name,' said Henry Isaiah, 'then I'll invent one. I shall call myself something smart and distinguished. I'll call myself James.'

'That's all right,' said Furless Fred, 'you can call yourself anything you like as long as everyone knows your new name.'

'How can I tell everyone my new name?' asked Henry Isaiah, who was now called James.

'Well, we could have a new name party for you and tell all the other toys at the party.'

'That's a very good idea,' said Rags. 'I shall send out the invitations at once. If I find Dog he'll be postman and take the invitations to everyone.'

Jane Hissey

James Bear, who used to be Henry Isaiah, went back happily to wait for his party invitation. He snuggled down under a blanket and dreamed of party hats and jellies and everyone calling him James. It would be the best party ever. Rags and Furless Fred carefully wrote out the invitations to everyone. They remembered to put James and not Henry Isaiah on Henry Isaiah's invitation and they gave them all to Dog to deliver. The next day everyone started arriving for the party. Nobody knew why they were having the party and some had brought presents in case it was anyone's birthday.

'It's a surprise party,' said Rags. 'Somebody wants to tell you something and he's going to tell you at the party.'

'Ooh,' said the toys, 'it sounds exciting.' Rabbit started to organize some games and soon everyone was having a lovely time. Rags and Furless Fred waited for James, who had been Henry Isaiah, to arrive, but he didn't. Soon everyone was hungry.

'Well, you'd better start on the food,' said Rags, peering out of the door to try and catch sight of the missing guest. Where could he be? They'd sent him an

invitation with the time and the place of the party. When everyone had finished their party food and begun to go home, Rags called Dog over. 'Dog,' he said, 'you did deliver all the invitations didn't you?'

'Of course I did,' said Dog, 'all except one.'

'Which one?' said Furless Fred and Rags at the same time.

'This one,' said Dog, producing a crumpled piece of paper he was carrying, 'it's addressed to someone called James. I asked everyone but nobody knew who that was.'

'Oh, no,' cried Rags, 'we forgot to tell Dog and now James, who was Henry Isaiah, has missed his own naming party.'

Rushing out of the room, they bumped straight into James. He was standing miserably, watching everyone going home from the party carrying balloons and pieces of cake. 'Was that my party?' he asked, sadly.

'Oh, James,' said Rags, 'I'm so sorry.' And he explained how Dog did not know where to take the invitation.

'Did I miss the games?' asked James.

'I'm afraid so,' said Rags.

'And the food?' asked James.

'And the food,' said Furless Fred.

AH HE

'All because I changed my name?' asked the very miserable bear.

'I'm afraid so,' said the others.

'Perhaps changing one's name is a bit risky,' said James, who was Henry Isaiah. 'I wouldn't want to miss any more parties, do you think perhaps I ought to change my name back to Henry Isaiah?'

'Perhaps that would be best,' said Rags, 'it's a very nice name you know, a very memorable name.'

'Yes, perhaps it isn't so bad,' said Henry Isaiah, who had briefly been James. 'Did you save me a balloon?'

'Of course we did,' said Furless Fred and Rags. 'Shall we write your name on it?' And they did. And Henry Isaiah proudly walked home with a big red balloon with 'Henry Isaiah' written on it.

Henry Isaiah is the right sort of name to have on a balloon, he thought to himself. It's nice and long and goes all the way round to the other side. It's twice as long as James.

THE CIRCUS

There had been a birthday party at the house where Old Bear and his friends lived. The big round table in the dining room had a big round cloth on it, and there, on top of the table was all the food that hadn't been eaten at the party. And there had been *so* much food, that an awful lot was still there. 'Just look at it all,' said Little Bear, 'we could have a feast if we could reach it.'

Unfortunately, all the chairs had been taken to another room for a game of musical chairs and there wasn't one to climb on to reach the food. Little Bear popped his head under the tablecloth to see whether there was a way up from the inside and squeaked with excitement. 'Look everyone!' he shouted, 'it's like a circus tent in here – a big top!'

The others popped their heads in too and soon all the toys had joined them. It really was like a huge, round tent. 'We could have a circus instead of a party,' said Bruno the big brown bear.

'How *do* you have a circus?' asked Little Bear.

'Well, everyone goes into the big top, or under the table in our case, and some people watch and some people do tricks.'

'And the people who watch have to clap and cheer,' added Sailor.

'It's a lovely idea,' said Rabbit. 'I could do jumping.'

'Jumping isn't a trick,' said Little Bear.

'It is if you jump very high or over something,' said Rabbit.

'Over what?' asked Little Bear.

'Rabbit could jump over me if he liked,' said Zebra, 'that would be a trick.'

Rabbit and Zebra practised their trick lots of times while the other toys discussed what they could do in the circus.

'I think I could juggle,' said Little Bear, 'almost.'

'And I could walk a tightrope,' said Sailor. 'If I could borrow your trousers,' he said to Little Bear, 'I could dress up as a clown, too.'

'That would be good,' said Bruno, 'but we need lots more acts. What can you do, Camel?'

'I don't know,' said Camel. 'If I ran round and round the big top, could someone balance on one of my humps?'

'We could try,' said Bruno.

Everyone had a go at standing up on Camel's humps. But nobody could do it except Rabbit, even when Camel stood still. Rabbit could stand on one leg, waggle his ears, hop up and down and even jump up in the air, whilst balancing on one of Camel's humps. Everyone was most impressed.

'You're good at tricks, aren't you,' said Bruno. 'What else can you do?'

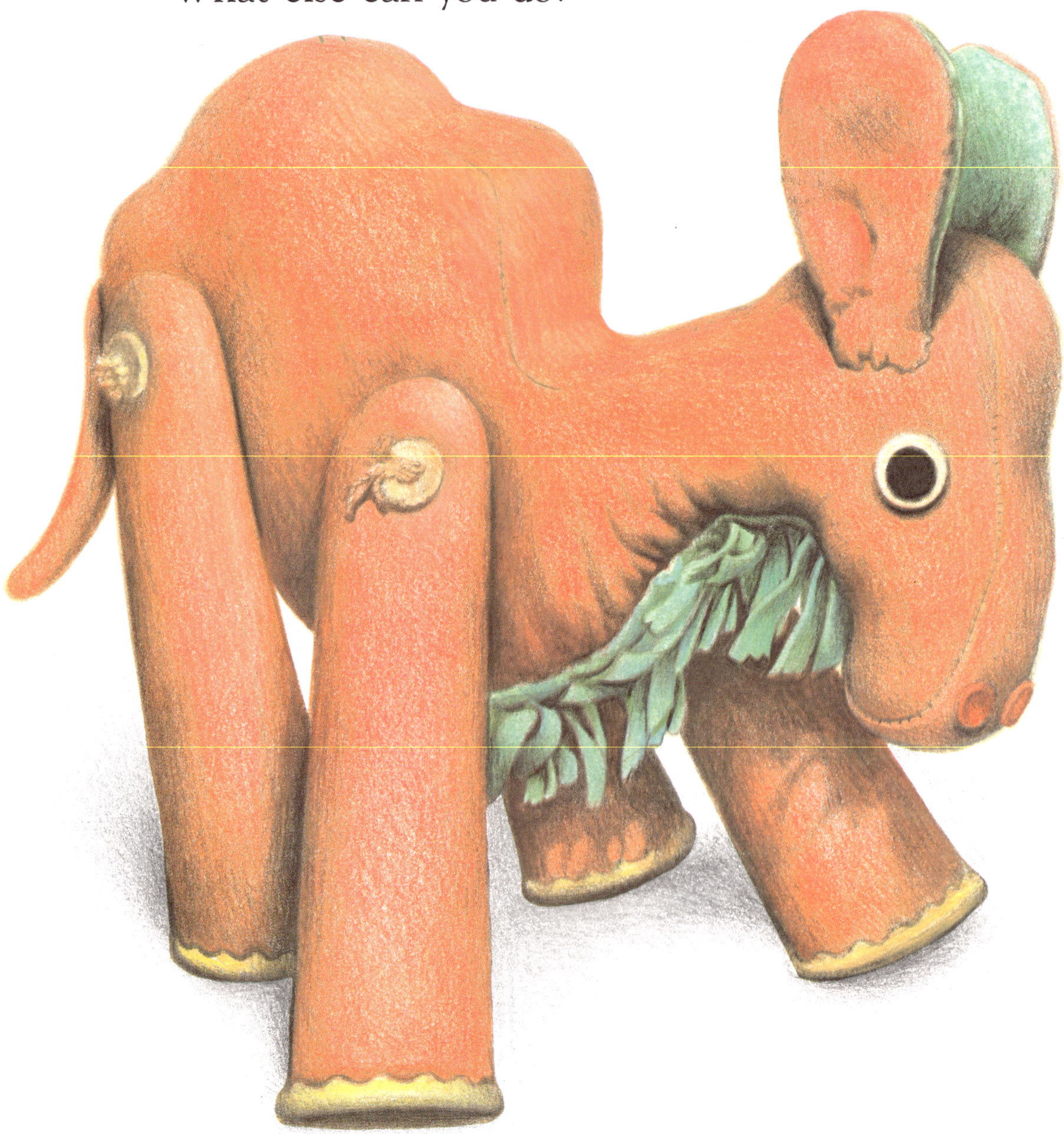

There was no doubt about it, Rabbit was going to be the star of the show. By the time he'd shown them how he could hang from things just by his feet, jump through a hoop, and juggle with three bean bags, the others all wanted to be the audience.

'We'll never be as good as Rabbit,' they all said.

'It doesn't matter,' said Bruno. 'Circuses are just meant to be fun. We don't really have to be good at everything.'

'Let's begin,' said Old Bear. He lifted a corner of the tablecloth to make an entrance, and all the toys marched in under the table. It was very exciting.

'I've never been to a circus, before,' said Duck.

'I don't think any of us have,' said Bruno, taking his place as ringmaster in the middle of the ring.

The toys all sat around the edge and Rabbit and Zebra stepped forward to do the first trick. Everyone clapped and cheered as Rabbit ran across the ring and leaped over Zebra's back. He landed on Old Bear's lap. But the other toys thought that was part of the trick. He did it a few more times until Bruno stopped him, and then Sailor came into the ring.

Sailor tied a skipping rope between two table legs and the toys watched excitedly as he carefully walked along the rope. He did fall off once, but he landed on one of the other toys, so he didn't hurt himself. Swinging himself back up again, he tried juggling this time while balancing.

'Well done!' called Old Bear. 'That's wonderful.'

It was Dog's turn next. He strolled into the ring balancing one of his rubber bones on his nose. 'I was going to balance two,' he said, 'but I couldn't remember where I buried the other one.'

Everyone clapped hard and he bowed and left the ring. And as he left, Camel came in. She trotted around the ring until Rabbit appeared and then, with Rabbit perched on a hump, she began to run really fast. Rabbit bounced about, standing first on one leg and then on the other. 'What shall I do for my next trick?' he called.

'Hop,' shouted one of the toys.

Camel thought they shouted, 'Stop,' and stopped so suddenly that Rabbit sailed through the air and hit the tablecloth. Grabbing wildly at it, he clung on and then, quite slowly, pulled the whole thing down. Plates of food landed all around the table and, in a second,

the circus tent had vanished. Rabbit, unhurt, wriggled out from under the cloth and looked at the food lying all around them. 'Oh dear,' he said, 'did I do that?'

'Never mind, Rabbit,' said Old Bear. 'We may have lost our circus but we found the feast. We never thought about pulling down the tablecloth to get all the food. Have a bun.'

'Oooh, I could juggle with these buns,' said Rabbit.

'Let's just eat them, shall we?' suggested Old Bear and, sitting under the table to eat, they enjoyed the food almost as much as they'd enjoyed the circus.